# *Swing Thoughts are for Sissies*

*1,111 things to think about when you shouldn't be thinking*

Tom Metz

 Whimpering Flagsticks Press

Copyright © 2013 by Thomas V. Metz, Jr.
All rights reserved.

Published by Whimpering Flagsticks Press,
Seattle, Washington.

No part of this publication may be reproduced, scanned or distributed in any print or electronic form without permission.

For information about special discounts for bulk purchases, please contact us through the website:
www.swingthoughts-sissies.com.

Metz, Thomas V., 1951-
Swing Thoughts are for Sissies : 1,111 things to think about when you shouldn't be thinking / Thomas V. Metz, Jr.

ISBN: 978-0-9898398-0-8

# Table of Contents

**Introduction** ............................................... 1
**Chipping** ..................................................... 5
   Ramblings—Right Knee ....................... 19
**Pitching** .................................................... 20
**Putting** ..................................................... 31
   Ramblings—Swing with Arms ........... 42
**Sand Shots** .............................................. 54
   Ramblings—Poor Tempo ..................... 62
**Full Swing** ............................................... 74
   Ramblings—Not Accelerating ............ 82
   Ramblings—Long Backswing Putt . 103
   Ramblings—Chipping with Wrists . 125
   Ramblings—Long Backswing Chip . 144
   Ramblings—Coiling & Uncoiling ..... 166
   Ramblings—Help Ball into Air ......... 186
**Practicing** .............................................. 200
   Ramblings—Having Fun ..................... 207

## Introduction

What I like about golf is that the ball always goes exactly where I hit it. This book will help you to like where you hit it more often.

Some people say you should have only one, or at most two, swing thoughts. Well, we will have none of that! As a contrarian, my philosophy is entirely different. I say the more the better. If one or two swing thoughts are good, 10 or 20 are really good, 50 are absolutely great, and 1,111 are nothing short of fantastic! Yep, you can never have too many swing thoughts.

All this talk about keeping the mind clear is completely wrong. If we were all Zen masters we would be too at peace to go aggravate ourselves with a round of golf. Swing thoughts are wonderful! Swing thoughts are the essence of golf. Without swing thoughts there is nothing; golf would be nothing!

For us golfers, that little subconscious is a powerful thing. It can override the conscious almost every time. So we need to whip that subconscious into shape, tell it what to do. The best way to do that is to be armed with some swing thoughts...like perhaps 1,111 of them! Your subconscious will not stand a chance.

Many of these swing thoughts may not resonate with you; but a few of them will. There even may be an "aha!" moment. Everybody is different. A swing thought that works for one person may not be helpful to another person. That is the beauty of golf; it is so individual. Peruse the list of thoughts and see which ones work for you. Of 1,111 swing thoughts there are probably a few that you will find helpful.

The book started out as a joke among my golf friends. They would tease me, saying that I had so many swing thoughts that I needed a database to keep track of them all. Being an analytical sort, this seemed quite natural to me. I don't know what their problem is. Anyway, I ended up with a lot of swing thoughts. So here they are.

You may notice that a number of swing ideas are repeated in the book. This is intentional. Some swing thoughts are too important not to mention multiple times. For example, keeping the right knee bent on the takeaway. The intent is to drive home the key concepts that are critical to the golf swing.

Reviewing a handful of swing thoughts every day is a pleasant and fruitful exercise. Who doesn't enjoy thinking about golf? Sometimes I lie in bed before falling asleep and my mind trundles over to golf. I visualize my swing. It is constructive and relaxing to review a few swing thoughts before drifting off.

Visualization can improve athletic performance in any sport, but particularly in golf. Read five or 10 tips a day and contemplate them. Create a picture in your mind. Imagine yourself doing the swing just like the tip says.

Picture your body moving that way.

When you wonder why the ball went where it did instead of where you wanted it to go, what should you do? Well, that's when you reach for this book and discover a passel of swing thoughts to solve your problem. No golf bag is complete without this book; no nightstand is complete without this book. One can never have too many swing thoughts.

## Count of swing thoughts

| | |
|---|---:|
| Chipping | 86 |
| Pitching | 59 |
| Putting | 126 |
| Sand Shots | 102 |
| Full Swing | 699 |
| Practice | <u>39</u> |
| Total: | 1,111 |

## Chipping

Pick a spot to land every chip.

---

Take three practice swings on chips.

---

Don't scoop the ball when chipping.

---

Put three-quarters of your weight on your left leg.

---

Make a sharp, descending strike on the ball.

---

Change the ball position to control how far the ball will go.

---

Pretend your hands are dead when you chip.

---

Follow through with a low finish.

---

Play the ball off your right heel.

---

Use your sand wedge for most chips.

---

On longer chips, chase the ball to the hole with the club head.

---

Alter the length of the back swing to control distance.

Keep the heel of the club off the ground when chipping from the fringe.

Let your wrists hinge naturally.

Keep your lower body quiet.

Turn your body through on all chips.

Hit down on the ball when chipping.

With a lob wedge, hinge your wrists quickly on the back swing.

Follow through, turning your chest to the target.

---

Don't let the club pass your hands.

---

For backspin, focus on hitting down on the ball, not behind it.

---

Pinch the ball against the turf.

---

Use a lower lofted club if you have more green to work with.

---

Loosen your grip pressure on chips.

---

Don't cock your wrists.

You must strike down on the ball, not scoop under it.

---

Make sure you hit the ball first, not the ground.

---

Use your putting grip for short chips.

---

Do not decelerate on chips.

---

Don't try to lift the ball off the ground.

---

Make a rhythmical swing, not jerky.

---

Let the club do the work.

Keep the face of the club pointing up after impact.

---

Be sure to accelerate through with the lob wedge.

---

Don't force a lob wedge; let the club weight control the speed.

---

Keep arms and wrists passive on chips.

---

Turn through faster or slower to determine distance.

---

Relax and commit to the shot.

From a few feet off the green, lift the heel of the club and swing like you are putting.

---

Set up for chips with your hands well ahead of the ball.

---

Keep the clubface slightly open on chips.

---

Play the ball way back in your stance.

---

Use your right arm to control your chip shots.

---

If you are several feet off the green, chip with a 7 or 8 iron.

On chips, the left wrist should stay flat at impact.

When chipping from the fringe, strike down on the ball.

Follow through on all chips.

Always accelerate on chips.

Use a more lofted club for a short chip.

On long chips, use a club with less loft.

Keep your hands ahead of the club head at impact.

---

Move your chest and arms in unison.

---

Use a slightly weaker grip on chips.

---

Make a strike down on the ball, not under the ball.

---

Chip with a short back swing and a longer follow-through.

---

Choke down 2 or 3 inches for more control on chips.

---

The body should turn forward along with the arms.

---

Don't try to help the ball into the air; let the club do it.

---

Chip with a 9 iron when two feet off the green.

---

On chips, make sure your hands are head of the ball at impact.

---

Do not use your wrists when chipping.

---

The length of your swing is determined by the length of the shot.

---

Don't take the club inside on the backswing for chips.

---

On short downhill chips, abbreviate your follow through.

---

Use a smooth tempo for all chips.

---

On hardpan, set up with the heel of the club off the ground.

---

Don't try to lift the ball up.

---

When putting from off the green with a 3 wood, choke down on the shaft.

---

In deep rough, hit behind the ball, just like you would in sand.

---

On short chips, use the same motion as your putting stroke.

---

Keep the left wrist firm through impact on chips.

---

Try chipping with the same grip as your putter grip.

---

Chip with your chin high and your back straight.

---

Restrict your follow-through for shorter chips.

---

Look at the front part of the ball when chipping.

---

Play the ball back in your stance when chipping from hardpan.

---

Stick your butt out on chips and putts.

---

Move your arms and shoulders as one unit.

---

When hitting from the rough around the green, commit to the shot.

---

When chipping, take a short backswing and accelerate.

---

Rock your shoulders and arms together when chipping.

---

Concentrate on making good contact with the ball.

---

When chipping with a low iron, choke down on the club.

---

Try to keep your wrists quiet.

---

Do not take a long backswing for a chip.

---

Use a more lofted club from the rough around the green.

## Ramblings: Number 1 Mistake—Straightening the Right Knee

Straightening the right knee when taking the club back is the biggest problem that amateurs make. The result is the transfer of your weight to the left side on the backswing. This is a reverse pivot. If your weight is already on your left side on the backswing, it is impossible to transfer the weight to your left leg when swinging down. There is no weight transfer and power is lost. I have several friends who golf this way and they hit weak drives. It is a difficult habit to change.

The fix is simple; just keep your right knee bent as you take the club back. Keep it bent the whole time. It is more athletic to swing when your right knee is bent than when your right knee is straight.

Swinging a club in slow motion is a good way to develop this habit. Now back to the swing thoughts.

## Pitching

Place the ball just forward of center with respect to your heels.

Keep the clubface open through impact.

Accelerate through as you swing.

When using a lob wedge, play the ball slightly forward in your stance.

Use a little wider stance with a lob wedge.

---

Your body should rotate around your left hip.

---

Approach the ball from the inside.

---

Grip down one inch on the club.

---

Quiet the lower body.

---

Keep your swing tempo the same for each shot.

---

Pinch the ball against the turf with short irons and wedge shots.

---

Don't quit on the shot.

---

Hit the ball with a descending blow.

---

Keep turning through the shot; don't stop.

---

Keep the club head low on the follow-through.

---

With the lob wedge, think about sliding the club just under the ball.

---

Close the clubface for a low, running shot.

---

On a short pitch, keep your stance narrow.

---

Keep your weight forward with the lob wedge.

---

Let the club do the work.

---

With a lob wedge, open the face and then lower the hands.

---

Maintain the wrist hinge on the downswing on short pitches.

---

Use an extra club or two when pitching to an elevated green.

---

Use a consistent tempo on all chips and pitches.

---

With a lob wedge, think about driving your right arm under the ball.

---

When hitting from tall grass, don't turn your right forearm over your left forearm.

---

For a half wedge shot, place the ball in the middle of your stance.

---

Be sure to turn your hips as you swing.

---

On a downhill shot, chase the ball down the slope.

For shorter distances, choke down and take a normal swing.

Keep your hands ahead of the ball at impact.

Use a slightly weaker grip with a lob wedge.

Focus on making good contact with the ball.

On short pitches, swing from 9 o'clock to 3 o'clock.

Put more weight on your left side for a shot from 40 to 60 yards.

With a lob wedge, keep the clubface pointing up after impact.

---

You are better off pitching from 100 yards than 50 yards; the ball will spin and stop.

---

Keep your head very still for shots with a lob wedge.

---

When pitching, open the clubface to make the ball fly higher and land softer.

---

Don't take the club back too far to the inside.

---

Use a consistent tempo on pitches.

---

Narrow your stance for short pitches.

---

For a shorter pitch, take the club back only to the 9 o'clock position.

---

Don't uncock your wrists too early on pitches.

---

To hit a high pitch shot, lower your hands at address.

---

Play the ball off the toe of your lob wedge.

When hitting a pitch, set up by letting your arms hang down naturally.

---

Turn your shoulders and arms together for a pitch.

---

Rotate your chest through and toward the target on pitches.

---

Use your sand wedge for pitch shots closer than 80 yards.

---

When hitting a pitch shot, you should pinch the ball against the ground.

---

Remember to hit down on the ball on pitch shots.

---

For a flop shot take a long slow full swing.

---

Your stance should be slightly open with your 9 iron and wedges.

---

Grip down a little for pitch shots.

---

Relax and swing smoothly.

---

For a short wedge shot, keep your weight on your left leg.

---

For a lob wedge shot, swing a little outside-in.

---

Use a three-quarter backswing for a 65 yard shot.

**Putting**

---

Keep your head directly over the ball.

---

The faster the green, the more break there will be.

---

Wet grass does not break as much.

---

Aim for an intermediate target, a foot in front of the ball.

---

Accelerate slightly through impact.

---

Let your arms hang easily under your shoulders.

---

Focus on controlling the speed of the putt.

---

On downhill putts, think about hitting the ball 50% or 70% of normal speed.

---

Be sure to accelerate on short putts.

---

Widen your stance when putting in wind.

---

Try giving more break than you normally would to avoid missing on the low side.

The putter should release just like an iron shot.

Keep your elbows in close on putts.

Never rush the stroke.

Let gravity help you with your putt.

Keep the putter low after impact.

On really long putts, take a longer backswing; do not swing faster.

Keep your head down on putts.

When putting put slightly more weight on your left leg.

---

Exhale during the forward stroke.

---

On long putts, accelerate smoothly.

---

Err on the higher side of the hole when reading the break.

---

Your eyes should be one inch inside the target line.

---

Lock your wrists.

Don't jab at the ball.

---

Swing back on a low, level path.

---

Hit up slightly on the ball to get it rolling nicely.

---

Your weight should be on the balls of your feet.

---

Keep your head still.

---

Swing back one-third and forward two-thirds.

---

A missed putt should go at least a foot past the cup.

---

On side-hill putts, break the shot down into two parts and then hit the first part.

---

Don't push the putter head through the ball.

---

Align your shoulders and feet parallel to the target line.

---

Swing from low to high.

---

Develop a rhythm for your putts...back and through.

---

Turn your chest as you swing.

---

Aim for the highest point of the break.

---

When putting, move your arms and shoulders together.

---

Begin reading the green as you are walking towards the green.

---

Open your stance a little on long putts.

---

When in doubt, always play for more break.

---

Let the club follow through and release.

---

Breathe a long breath before the putt.

---

Keep your arms and chest in synch as you swing.

---

Keep your hands ahead of the ball as you swing the putter.

---

Think…the ball wants to go in the hole.

---

Walk up to the hole to feel the green with your feet on every putt.

---

Don't let your hands get involved in the putt.

---

Use the same routine for every putt.

---

Don't break your wrists during the putt.

---

Take the putter back just a little bit; the shorter the backswing, the better.

---

Relax your shoulders.

---

Don't move your head during your putt.

---

Swing slower on downhill putts.

A putt will often break toward the water.

---

Speed is more important than direction.

---

The ball is not moving, the hole is not moving; how hard could this be?

---

Use the putter to roll the ball to the hole.

---

Putt by taking the minimum backswing necessary and then follow through.

---

Always try to have consistent speed on your putts.

Watch the ball as you make contact.

# Ramblings: Number 2 Mistake— Swinging with your Arms

When I watch people at the driving range, about 90% of them make their golf swings primarily with their arms. This is natural because we use our arms for many of our activities—such as hammering a nail, sawing a board, painting the house, washing the car; you get the idea. It is not a natural thing to swing a golf club with your upper body and arms moving together. It is a learned thing.

But it is not hard to learn. Simply practice swinging your arms and chest together. There is a drill that you may have seen that involves holding the golf club with the handle against your chest and your arms straight out. Then you turn back and through moving your arms and chest together. It takes some practice but is not a difficult thing.

Always read putts from below the hole, not above the hole.

---

Don't look up until the ball has gone six feet from you.

---

Relax after setting up.

---

The slower the ball rolls the more the break will affect it.

---

Hit short putts firmly to take away the break.

---

Don't ever be afraid to putt. You love to putt.

Be sure to accelerate through the ball on uphill putts.

Study the last five feet of the putt because that is where it will break the most.

The speed of the putt determines how much it will break.

Vary the length of the backswing to get the right distance.

Always putt with confidence. Why not?

On long putts, aim for a three-foot circle around the hole.

---

Make firm contact through the ball.

---

Swing by turning your shoulders around your spine.

---

Let your arms hang down naturally.

---

Concentrate on speed more than the line of the putt.

---

Roll your putts; don't push through them.

---

Don't hunch over.

Don't flick your wrists on putts.

Rhythm and tempo are critical on putts.

On a long putt, pick a spot four feet away and aim there.

Rock your arms and shoulders as one unit.

Visualize the line you want the putt to follow as you swing.

Think about how far back to take the putter.

---

Make sure your feet are square to the target line.

---

Your wrists should not bend during the putting stroke.

---

Use a nice even tempo as you swing back and through.

---

Do not jab at the ball.

---

Bend at the hips.

---

Set up with your feet parallel to the hole, not aiming at the hole.

On long putts, do not swing fast or rush it.

---

Follow through beyond your left hip.

---

On downhill putts, use lighter grip pressure.

---

Don't take too big of a back swing with the putter.

---

Keep your left wrist firm throughout the stroke.

---

Pretend you are confident, even if you are not.

---

Swing smoothly back and through on long putts.

---

Take just one practice swing.

---

Try using a shorter backswing to increase accuracy.

---

Press your hands forward when setting up to putt.

---

When putting, let the shoulders and arms do most of the work.

---

Accelerate through impact on every putt.

---

A shorter putting stroke is usually better.

---

Divide a double breaking putt into several sections.

---

For an uphill putt, pretend the hole is farther away.

---

Stand up taller for long putts.

---

For very long putts, use a slight wrist cock.

---

Choke down on the grip when putting on a fast green.

Hitting the putt on the toe of the club will deaden the putt.

Take a short backswing on putts and follow through.

Stick your butt out a little when setting up for a putt.

For putts 15 feet and shorter, your ball should always go past the hole unless it drops in.

Be relaxed and set up comfortably for every putt.

For downhill putts, pretend the hole is closer than it really is.

---

Remember that downhill putts will break more than uphill putts.

---

For a downhill putt, swing a little slower.

---

Putt by simply rocking your shoulders.

---

Let the putter swing freely.

---

Take the putter back low to the ground.

---

Focus on a spot on the ball before you swing the putter.

---

Think more about how hard to hit the ball than the perfect line.

---

Never, ever decelerate on a putt.

---

The ball position should be a little bit forward.

---

Watch the ball roll past the hole to read the break for the next putt.

---

## Sand Shots

Play the ball forward in your stance so the club strikes the sand first.

———

Hit one or two inches of sand behind the ball.

———

Open the clubface and aim a little left.

———

Make a full finish with sand shots.

———

Do not hit down on sand shots.

———

Put your weight on the inside of your left foot.

---

Keep a firm left wrist through impact.

---

On a downhill lie, follow through down the slope.

---

Use a sand wedge, not a lob wedge, and open the face.

---

Rotate your hips and torso through the shot.

---

Shift your weight forward as you swing.

---

With only one foot in the sand, swing with your arms only.

---

Swing the club level at impact.

---

Hinge your wrists fully on sand shots.

---

In the sand, play the ball farther forward, off your left heel.

---

On a buried lie, bend your knees more.

---

Set up with your hands low in a bunker.

---

From a long greenside bunker shot, make sure to release the club.

---

Follow through, follow through, follow through.

---

Accelerate your swing when in the sand.

---

In fairway bunkers, try sweeping the ball.

---

Rotate the clubface open to hit a shorter shot.

---

Rotate the clubface closed to get more distance.

---

Swing through and accelerate.

---

Open your stance a little and swing along your stance line.

---

A full swing sand wedge shot will go one-third as far as a regular sand wedge shot.

---

Keep your swing speed consistent.

---

In downhill sand, tilt your shoulders to match the slope.

---

Swing down and under the ball, not down and up.

---

To hit a high sand shot, swing through at a higher speed.

---

If the ball is above your feet, play it back in your stance.

---

In wet or hard sand, do not open the clubface; dig the leading edge under the ball.

---

For a high and short shot, open the clubface even more.

---

Point the grip of the club just to the right of your belt buckle at set-up.

---

Widen your stance in the sand.

Turn your chest toward the target as you swing.

---

With a thin lie in sand, use a pitching wedge to avoid bouncing the club off the sand.

---

Follow through high to your left shoulder.

---

Don't flip your wrists.

---

For a longer shot, follow through more.

---

At set-up, the club should be parallel to your left leg.

Select a spot to land the ball on the fly.

# Ramblings: Number 3 Mistake — Poor Tempo

When I watch a good golfer, I am always impressed by their great tempo. Some swing fairly slowly, some swing relatively fast and some are in the middle, but their tempo is always smooth. Back and through. There is no rush.

I have learned to take the club back more slowly because then I don't do bad things at the top. This has helped my tempo because prior to this adjustment I was swinging too fast.

Some golf pros tell students to pause briefly at the top and other pros do not think this is a good idea. It doesn't really matter as far as tempo is concerned. I like the phrase 'slow from the top' because it promotes good tempo. You can't learn tempo from a book so I have no intention of trying to describe how to do it. Just work on it.

Grip the club more in your palm on sand shots so the shot is not too wristy.

---

The more you open the clubface, the more you should open your stance.

---

Use a shallower swing plane on sand shots.

---

Set up with the ball forward in your stance.

---

Swing with a shallow arc if the ball is above your feet.

---

Open your stance in wet sand.

With a high lip, play the ball more forward in your stance.

---

The bottom of the club head should contact the sand first, not the leading edge.

---

Swing hard on sand shots, especially if there is a high lip.

---

Do not unhinge your wrists too early.

---

Accelerate on the downswing in sand.

---

Swing faster or slower for higher or lower ball flight.

Let the club do the work.

---

Keep your feet apart when in sand.

---

You want a quiet lower body in sand.

---

Let the club release when on a down slope.

---

In the sand, the club head should pass your hands before it gets to the ball.

---

Use a pitching wedge or 9 iron for a longer bunker shot.

---

Stay aggressive on sand shots.

---

In sand, skim the club under the ball.

---

With a buried lie in sand, close the clubface.

---

On sand shots, hold the clubface open as you swing through.

---

In wet sand, keep the clubface more closed.

---

Always make a full follow-through from the sand.

---

On firm sand, keep your weight forward.

---

On bunker shots, make sure to keep the club moving through impact.

---

Use a weaker grip when hitting from sand.

---

Choke down a little when hitting from a bunker.

---

Keep your left knee bent slightly in the sand.

---

For a 40-yard bunker shot, use your 8 or 9 iron, not your sand wedge.

---

Your swing path should be from out to in when hitting from sand.

---

Keep accelerating through on your sand shots.

---

Put most of your weight on your left leg when hitting from sand.

---

Control the distance of a sand shot by how fast you turn your body through.

---

For a short bunker shot, open the clubface and have a short follow through.

---

Align your feet slightly left of your target when hitting from a bunker.

Keep the clubface square for a long bunker shot.

For a high bunker shot, open your feet 30° and open up the clubface.

Take a wide stance when hitting from a downhill lie in a bunker.

Choke down on the club with an uphill lie in a bunker.

Open the clubface and take a long shallow divot in the sand.

In the sand, the club head should get to the ball before your hands.

---

In wet sand, use a 60° lob wedge and choke down.

---

With a fried-egg lie, use a steep downswing and more wrist hinge.

---

Keep your head still when hitting from the sand.

---

Squat down a little when setting up for a sand shot.

---

Swing aggressively on most sand shots.

---

In the sand, take a wider stance with more knee flex.

---

In a deep bunker, use a more vertical backswing.

---

Do not uncock your wrists too early in the sand.

---

Use your pitching wedge when hitting from sand near the lip of the bunker.

---

The pace of your swing determines distance when hitting from a bunker.

---

With a downhill lie in a bunker, swing the club down the slope.

In a bunker, play the ball forward in your stance so you can easily hit behind it.

Choke down when hitting from a fairway bunker.

Take a three-quarter backswing when hitting from a fairway bunker.

With a plugged lie, swing down on a steeper path.

Keep your lower body more still when hitting sand shots.

Make sure you have enough club-head speed to get the ball to the hole.

Make a full turn for a long green-side bunker shot.

## The Full Swing

Keep your right knee bent on the backswing.

---

Make sure your head is behind the ball.

---

Let the club do the work.

---

Keep your chin up.

---

As you swing, force your left heel down.

---

The takeaway should be low and slow.

---

Keep your left arm straight.

---

Grip the club lightly.

---

Visualize the finish position.

---

Coil by turning your hips as far as they will turn and keep the right knee bent.

---

Start the downswing by moving the left knee to the left.

---

Maximize your weight transfer through the ball.

Swing inside out.

---

Pause at the top.

---

For good rhythm, say "and….through" as you swing.

---

Put your left shoulder under your chin.

---

Imagine the triangle of arms and shoulders, back and through.

---

Hands loose and relaxed.

---

On the backswing, place your left shoulder over the right knee.

---

Do not sway to the right; coil instead.

---

Turn your shoulders on the takeaway, don't tilt them.

---

On upslope shots, position your shoulders level with the slope.

---

Keep your left arm close to chest.

---

Start the swing by letting the club drop.

---

Rotate the forearms, crossing them over as you swing.

---

Keep your left heel on the ground.

---

Shift your weight and step into the ball.

---

Extend both arms just after impact.

---

Turn your right hip forward and up just as you hit the ball.

---

Pretend the ball is made of Styrofoam to promote a smooth swing.

---

Keep your right elbow near your right side.

Put about 90% of your weight on your right foot at the top of your backswing.

On the downswing, transfer your weight to your left side.

Clear your hips out of the way so your arms can swing freely.

Roll your right hand over your left at impact.

Swing using only 80% power with your driver.

Turn your body toward the fairway for the correct follow-through.

---

Visualize a nice follow-through.

---

The left eye should be just back of the ball.

---

Swing the hands through on the path you want the ball to travel.

---

The ball goes where the hands go.

---

Play the ball off the toe when hitting the lob wedge.

---

Swing with relaxed arms and wrists.

---

Keep the club head in front of your body on the takeaway.

---

Make a full arm extension through impact.

---

Rotate your chest toward the target.

---

Use an abbreviated finish on a knockdown shot.

---

Accelerate the club through impact.

---

Allow your head to move a little as you swing.

# Ramblings: Number 4 Mistake—Not Accelerating Past Impact

Accelerating the club is one of the most magical moves that we can do with any golf swing. It is critical to accelerate through the ball on every shot: drives, long irons, short irons, chips and putts. Swing slowly from the top and then gradually accelerate. This is an excellent way to hit a golf ball. Accelerating will also help your putting and chipping.

The club head should continue to accelerate after impact. This is not a hit; it is a swing. That is why this book is about "swing thoughts," not "hitting thoughts." The ball just happens to get in the way of your swing. Too many golfers think about it as a hit. You can see them at the practice range--hit, hit, hit.

Swinging, rather than hitting, is a different mental picture. Don't hit *at* the ball, swing *through* the ball. And the best way to hit through the ball is to continue accelerating the club past the ball. Give it a try; it actually works great.

Keep your arm swing synchronized with your body turn.

---

When your body stops turning on the backswing, your arms should stop too.

---

Keep your hips turning level through the swing.

---

On upslope shots, swing along the surface of the slope.

---

On the downswing, rotate your right forearm down and into your side.

---

Hit down on the inside of the ball.

Start the swing with the left hip; bump it back and left.

---

Keep your head still.

---

Rotate your hips all the way through impact.

---

Aim at a spot five feet beyond the ball.

---

Let your hands release after you have struck the ball.

---

Start the downswing from the ground up.

Hinge your wrists and maintain that position as you turn to the top.

Keep the club out, but the left arm in.

Your hips should end up over the left foot after the swing.

Rotate your right shoulder down as you hit.

Think—"left shoulder...right shoulder."

On a tight lie, trap the ball between the club and the ground.

Take a shorter backswing with wedges to control distance.

For a draw, place the ball back in your stance.

Crack the whip through impact.

Choke down on shots within 120 yards to get correct distance.

Turn so your back faces the target.

The left hand should be leading at impact.

Take a tall stance in a fairway bunker.

---

Shift your weight from right to left as you swing.

---

Your right side should stay lower than the left side.

---

In deep rough, hinge the wrists quickly and swing down steeply.

---

Use the same swing for long irons as you do for a wedge.

---

Set up with shoulders parallel to target line.

---

Close your stance to hit a draw.

---

Turn your left foot out to allow more hip turn.

---

Make a smooth weight shift.

---

Clear your left hip on the downswing.

---

Finish in a balanced position.

---

Stay loose and swing freely.

---

Drive the right shoulder down and through the ball.

At the top, the shaft should be parallel with the target line.

Tee the ball higher for a draw.

Don't try to swing too hard.

Follow through completely and in a flowing motion.

Don't make your hips too active on the downswing.

Keep your spine angle the same at impact.

Continue rotating your right shoulder through until it points at the target.

---

Stay on plane on the backswing.

---

At the top, your shoulders should be behind the ball.

---

Don't have too much tension in your arms.

---

Too narrow a stance will restrict hip turn.

---

Make a full shoulder turn.

---

Don't let the club pass the hands at impact.

---

Maintain flex in the knee as your weight shifts right.

---

Don't start the downswing with your arms.

---

Pull the club back with your right shoulder.

---

For a draw, aim right and toe in the club.

---

Finish low for a penetrating shot into the wind.

---

Shift your weight to the right on the backswing.

———————————————

To curve the ball right, aim your body to the left.

———————————————

To curve the ball left, aim your body to the right.

———————————————

Keep your head behind the ball through impact.

———————————————

Tee the ball lower for a fade.

———————————————

The toe of the club should pass the heel as it releases.

———————————————

Do not cast the club by coming over the top.

---

Let your arms follow as you swing.

---

If between clubs, choke down on the longer club and swing aggressively.

---

Keep the club moving through impact.

---

Don't bend over too far.

---

Stay fluid through the ball.

---

Place your weight on the balls of your feet, not your heels.

Think about your swing plane as you swing.

---

Keep hips level on the turn away; don't tilt them.

---

Don't get your hands too close to your body.

---

In wind, move the ball back in your stance.

---

Finish with your right shoulder under your chin.

---

Keep your lower body quiet on fairway bunker shots.

---

Don't sway to the left as you swing.

---

Let your arms hang freely in front of you.

---

Keep the club on the right arc.

---

Don't dip past parallel at the top.

---

Create resistance on the right side.

---

Maintain soft arms on the short irons.

---

Don't force the shot; let it go.

Flex your knees just before you swing back.

Show your back to the target on takeaway.

Move the ball back in your stance to make good contact with short irons.

As you turn through, keep your elbows close together.

Take the club back slowly; there is no hurry.

Keep your hands away from your head at the top.

---

Widen your stance in windy conditions.

---

Plant your feet solidly in fairway bunkers.

---

Stay calm at the top.

---

Extend your arms fully on the backswing.

---

Complete your backswing before starting your downswing.

---

Concentrate on rhythm throughout the swing.

---

Swing long irons the same way as short irons.

---

The club head should continue to accelerate after impact.

---

On wedge shots, pinch the ball off the turf.

---

Try to achieve a free release of the club head.

---

Keep your hands cocked as you swing down.

---

As you start down, press on the ball of your left foot.

---

Contact the ball before the sand when in a fairway bunker.

---

Swing freely and with even tempo.

---

Don't get your right arm trapped behind your body.

---

On long irons, keep your lower body as still as possible.

---

Roll your forearms with the lob wedge.

---

Think "rhythm" just before taking the club back.

---

End with your right shoulder over your left leg.

---

Keep your butt out and your back straight.

---

Relax your grip.

---

For a draw, fold your right arm over your left on the follow-through.

---

Tilt slightly to your right at set-up.

---

At set-up, bend your knees a little and bend from the hips.

---

Pull your shoulder blades together at the top.

---

Swing with an inside path to the ball.

---

Take one less club on a downhill lie.

---

Uncoil from the ground up.

---

The ball should be in the center of your stance in a fairway bunker.

---

Pull the club with your legs and trunk, not the hands.

Do not straighten the right knee on the backswing.

When hitting from tall grass, aim more right since the grass will grab the club head.

When in doubt always take more club.

On the takeaway, keep the left arm in.

Start the downswing by bumping left with your left hip.

# Ramblings: Number 5 Mistake—Putting with a Long Backswing

Taking too big a backswing is the number one putting mistake. It is better to take a short backswing and then swing forward with slight acceleration and follow through. The idea is to take as little backswing as possible.

One time I tried to teach a friend this trick by putting my foot right behind his putter. He could not swing back at all and it was interesting to see his reaction. He froze and could not putt. Finally, he got the idea. He swung the putter with minimal backswing.

This is a good way to develop a short backswing. Try putting with *no* backswing. And I mean no backswing, zip, zero, nil, not even an inch. You should swing about twice as far on the forward swing as you do on the backswing. This is particularly effective for short putts, about three or four feet. We usually accelerate on long putts but not on short putts. Give it a try.

On a knockdown shot, make sure to extend your arms through impact.

---

Don't straighten up at the top.

---

Adjust for distance by changing the length of your backswing.

---

Swing through, not down, with the driver.

---

When hitting from a divot, position the ball back in your stance.

---

Don't swing harder on long bunker shots.

Rotate your hips until they meet resistance.

On a downwind shot, spin the ball more than usual.

Visualize fluid motion.

For a fade, hold off on releasing the club.

Do not start the downswing with the upper body.

Transfer your weight to the left and unwind the hips.

Let your hands and arms drop naturally.

---

Move your right side completely through the shot.

---

Swing easier when into the wind.

---

Keep your shoulders and arms connected on takeaway.

---

When hitting from a divot, use a descending blow.

---

Use a three-quarter swing from fairway bunkers.

The left shoulder should turn down and under your chin, to maintain spine angle.

Hit with the right palm facing downward with fairway woods.

Set up for the driver with the ball opposite the left arm pit.

Your arms should hang directly under your shoulders.

Keep your right knee bent to prevent the hips from turning too far.

In tall grass, set up with more weight on the left leg.

---

Start the downswing with a shift of your hips to the left.

---

With your 3 wood, sweep the ball off the turf.

---

With a tight lie, think about a low finish.

---

Take the club back with your body, not your hands.

---

Turn your shoulders as far as possible.

---

Keep your weight on the inside of your right foot on the backswing.

---

Tilt your right knee in at address.

---

Feel slight tension in your left shoulder at the top of the backswing.

---

The 'V's of your thumb and first finger should point to your right shoulder.

---

Fire your hips for power.

---

When setting up for the driver, tilt your spine away from the target.

---

Keep your weight on the right side and right heel.

---

The left side of your body should initiate the downswing.

---

Set up for a 3 wood with the ball two inches inside of the left heel.

---

Keep your legs quiet on the downswing.

---

In tall grass, use a steep angle to hit down on the ball.

---

With irons, squeeze the ball down against the grass.

Do not straighten your right leg during the backswing.

---

Keep the club head traveling down the target line as long as possible with the 3 wood.

---

Don't use a sand wedge for a long bunker shot.

---

In heavy rough, hinge your wrists early.

---

For a knockdown shot, go up two clubs.

---

Make a downward strike with the hybrid club.

---

For a fade, move the ball slightly forward.

---

Make a complete turn.

---

Get your shoulders turned and weight shifted.

---

With the driver, hit the ball on the upswing.

---

Shorten your backswing in the wind.

---

On the takeaway, feel your weight move to your right heel.

---

With irons, your weight should be distributed equally over the middle of your feet.

---

Do not grip the club too tightly.

---

Your hips should shift laterally at first, then start to rotate.

---

Get loose by swinging two clubs for 20 swings.

---

To hit a higher shot widen your stance and put the ball forward.

---

Swing down the slope with a downhill lie.

---

Take more club to avoid coming up short.

---

Begin the downswing by pushing down on your left foot.

---

Aim the face of the club before setting your feet.

---

Finish with your belt buckle facing the target.

---

Ignore the club striking the ball and just visualize a good swing.

On a long bunker shot, use a lower lofted club.

In the wind take one or two extra clubs.

Open your stance on long bunker shots.

When hitting down wind, use a full swing.

Be sure to follow through when in heavy rough.

Increase your wrist hinge on your backswing for more power.

Turn completely on the backswing.

Aim for contact with the ball on the inside quarter of the ball.

For a draw, position the ball slightly back in your stance.

Hinge the club early in tall grass.

Lead with your hands on iron shots.

On a knockdown shot, do not re-hinge your wrists after impact.

Treat a long bunker shot just like any other shot.

---

Use one more club when hitting from a divot.

---

Take one more club on an uphill lie.

---

Make sure your posture is correct before every shot.

---

Don't hunch over with your back.

---

After shifting the hips left to start the downswing, unwind your hips.

---

With iron shots, focus on the front half of the ball.

---

Keep your hands relaxed at address.

---

Point the butt of the club at the target line as you swing down.

---

Initiate the downswing with your left knee.

---

Your hips should not sway on the backswing.

---

Keep your right elbow in when hitting a drive.

---

Don't lift up when you swing back.

---

A light grip allows you to release the club head through the ball.

---

Pinch the ball against the ground with a tight lie.

---

The insides of your feet should be as wide as the outsides of your shoulders.

---

Don't even think about straightening your right leg on the backswing.

---

Keep your wrist angle when you hit in tall grass.

---

Keep your butt out on the set-up.

---

Don't use a sand wedge from a tight lie.

---

Hit the low stinger with a 3 iron or with the driver.

---

Your last thought should be rhythm.

---

Do not slide to the right on the backswing.

---

Tuck your left shoulder under your chin on the backswing.

---

Keep the L-shape between forearm and club as long as possible.

---

On iron shots, think about squeezing the ball against the turf.

---

Try to touch your forearms together as you swing through.

---

Aim your feet parallel to the target line, not directly at the target.

---

On the backswing, try to put your hands as far away from your head as you can.

---

On long irons, use a flatter swing, not a steep backswing.

---

Keep your spine angle the same as you swing back and through.

---

For more control, grip down.

---

Don't bend your knees too much.

---

Pay attention to tempo on all shots.

---

As you swing, rotate your left thigh and turn the hips through.

---

Relax your shoulders.

---

Swing every club with the same rhythm.

For a draw, use a stronger grip, turning your left hand clockwise.

For more spin, use an open stance and open up the clubface.

Make sure that your head is behind the ball at impact.

Rotate the forearms as you swing through.

Point the handle of the club at the ball as you swing down.

Always aim for an intermediate target.

---

Don't lift the club too sharply on your backswing.

---

## Ramblings: Number 6 Mistake— Chipping with Your Wrists

Ahhh, those pesky wrists! They are troublesome aren't they? They always want to get into the act.

If you are a superb athlete with exceptional hand eye coordination, then fine, chip with your wrists. Fuzzy Zoeller is a good example. He has wonderful touch and magic wrists. But we are not all Fuzzy.

The best way to consistently hit good chips is to simply rock your shoulders and arms together and keep your wrists quiet.

Swing from the inside to the outside.

---

Don't place your hands too far away from your body at set-up.

---

Hinge your wrists after the club reaches your hips.

---

On a side hill lie, with the ball below your feet, swing more vertically.

---

First shift your weight to your left leg, and then turn your hips.

---

Don't cast the club, i.e., don't release your wrists too early at the top.

---

Follow through with your arms and hands toward the target.

---

For a fade, open the clubface slightly.

---

Fire your hips through impact.

---

Tee the ball up lower for a low stinger shot.

---

Make a slow, smooth takeaway with the driver.

---

Bend from your hips; don't slouch over.

Use more club than you think for almost every shot.

---

Keep the club just short of parallel at the top of the backswing.

---

Keep your head down.

---

Put your weight on the inside of your right leg on the backswing.

---

Watch the ball closely as you hit it.

---

Make sure your shoulders are aligned with the target line at set-up.

Keep consistent speed on every shot.

---

Turn your back to the target on the backswing.

---

Keep your right elbow in close to your side on the downswing.

---

For more power, delay turning your shoulders until your hips are unwinding.

---

For a knockdown shot, choke down on the club and take a shorter backswing.

---

Push your right knee toward the left knee on the downswing.

Release the club after impact.

---

Hold the club in your fingers, not in the palm.

---

Once your shoulders stop turning back, your arms should too.

---

Follow through forward, not around.

---

Make sure your downswing is not too steep.

---

Don't grip the club too tightly.

Waggle the club to stay loose.

---

Don't swing too fast.

---

Use your rotation to raise the club, don't lift it up.

---

As you swing, think about driving your right knee into the ball.

---

Have a specific target in mind for each shot; don't just hit it down the middle.

---

Do not straighten your right leg on the backswing.

---

For a draw, close the clubface slightly.

---

When punching out, grip more tightly with your left hand.

---

Relax your hands at the top.

---

Think about keeping the same swing plane throughout your swing.

---

With the driver, take the club away in a wide arc.

---

Never try to swing too fast.

---

Stay in balance throughout your swing.

---

Use the same routine to set up for every shot.

---

On tight fairways, hit a low stinger.

---

Don't look up as soon as you hit the ball.

---

Let the club do the work.

---

Play the ball in the middle of your stance for a low stinger.

---

Keep your arms and torso connected as you take the club away.

---

Concentrate on making solid contact with the ball.

---

Trust your swing.

---

Follow through low, through the ball; do not lift up.

---

For a draw or fade, always swing along the path of your foot alignment.

---

Coil first with your shoulders and then turn your hips.

---

Let your wrists cock naturally; don't force them.

---

Swing the club with no tension.

---

The best swing path is slightly inside out.

---

Keep your hands high on the backswing.

---

Concentrate on the swing path.

---

Take the club away slowly and smoothly.

---

Don't muscle the shot; just let it unwind.

---

Avoid any kind of swaying during the shot.

---

Make sure the ball is not too far forward or too far back at set-up.

---

Keep the right elbow in front of the right hand on the downswing.

---

Use a neutral grip with the palms facing each other.

---

For irons, hit down on the ball; don't try to scoop under it.

---

Do not uncoil your shoulders too quickly.

---

The right arm should be higher than the left when the club is half way back.

---

Make sure the club is square at impact.

---

Make a full turn on every shot.

---

Keep your hands ahead of the club head at impact.

---

On the downswing, try to keep a 90-degree angle with your arms as long as you can.

Initiate the backswing by turning your shoulders.

---

Hit most shots with only 80% power.

---

Keep your chin up for good posture.

---

The arms should flow straight forward to the target.

---

Swing through the ball, not at the ball.

---

Keep light pressure with your grip.

---

Don't flip your wrists.

---

After impact, extend the club down the target line.

---

Use a steeper swing angle in the rough.

---

Tempo is the most important part of the swing.

---

Make sure to rotate around your spine.

---

Follow through on every shot.

---

Remember that it is a swing, not a hit.

Do not rush on the downswing.

---

Let the hands cross over after impact.

---

Commit to the shot.

---

Take the club back nice and slow.

---

Don't try to scoop the ball with short irons.

---

Keep your back straight and let your arms hang down naturally.

---

Shift your weight to the right leg on the backswing.

---

Take one practice swing to monitor your tempo.

---

Concentrate on having the right position at the top.

---

Roll your left hand over after impact.

---

Don't hunch over with your back.

---

Use the same pre-shot routine every time.

---

Keep your arms and body in synch.

Drop your hands to start your downswing.

On a downhill lie, set your feet farther apart.

Keep your head and chin up.

Never rush at the top.

Point your right elbow at your right hip on the downswing.

Maintain your wrist hinge as you start down.

Keep your left heel on the ground during the backswing.

On the takeaway the club head should be out in front of the body.

Keep your right elbow close to your right side on the downswing.

# Ramblings: Number 7 Mistake—Chipping with a Long Backswing

I don't know why people take such long backswings when chipping, but it is very common. This is not a good way to chip. A long backswing encourages deceleration which is always bad.

You should accelerate on all chips. Take a short backswing and accelerate a little bit with a long follow-through. Nothing but good stuff happens when you do this.

Drop into the 'slot' on the downswing.

On side hill lies, choke down on the club.

In downhill rough, make sure your hands are ahead of the ball.

Keep the club head on plane.

Your spine should tilt away from the ball at address.

The right leg should turn forward through impact.

---

Turn your left foot out about 15 degrees.

---

Swing smoother with the driver.

---

Point the club parallel to the target at the top.

---

Come through with your right hip as you hit.

---

Pause very slightly at the top.

---

Do not slide your lower body forward during the shot.

---

Keep your left elbow close to your chest.

---

At impact your hands should lead the club head.

---

For a draw, toe the club in and swing along your stance line.

---

In a fairway bunker, play the ball slightly back in your stance.

---

In wind, stand back farther from the ball so you can swing around more.

---

Have only one swing thought per swing. (You've got to be kidding!)

Always make a complete backswing.

Start your downswing slowly.

When hitting a wedge from the rough, keep the clubface firm through impact.

For more spin, play the ball farther back in your stance.

When between clubs, swing softer with the longer club.

Keep your right wrist cocked as long as possible.

Your left shoulder should be higher than your right at address.

---

From hard pack, keep your lower body quiet.

---

For power, coil against your flexed right knee.

---

On an upslope shot, keep your shoulders parallel to the slope.

---

Don't separate your arms from your body.

---

Tuck your shoulder under your chin on the backswing.

Push off your right foot for more power.

Stay down as you hit through the shot.

Turn your chest through impact.

Maintain rhythm in your downswing.

As you follow through, your right shoulder should point at the target.

Take one more club when playing in the rain.

Turn your chest and arms through together.

———

Relax your shoulders and arms.

———

Align your feet, hips and shoulders parallel to the target.

———

Keep some bend in your right knee as you swing back.

———

Swing wide on the backswing with your driver.

———

Make sure you are balanced and centered at set-up.

———

Turn your left shoulder behind the ball.

---

Start your downswing with your hips.

---

In rough, play the ball back in your stance slightly.

---

Make sure your knees are flexed at set-up.

---

Keep your arms connected to your chest.

---

Maintain the triangle of your arms and shoulders throughout the swing.

---

Do not take any sand before you hit the ball in a fairway bunker.

---

Release the club head down the target line.

---

Do not ever reverse pivot.

---

Keep a firm grip when hitting from long rough.

---

Use timing, not effort, to get power.

---

Turn your left armpit as far as you can.

---

As you swing down, keep your hands low and the club head high.

---

Pick a specific target for every shot.

---

Rotate your right forearm through impact.

---

The first move on your downswing should not be hurried.

---

Don't over-control the club.

---

For power keep your right elbow in front of your hip as you swing.

---

Pause briefly at the top of your swing.

Proper tempo will solve a lot of problems.

---

Put more weight on your left side when hitting from a fairway bunker.

---

Don't drag the club through.

---

Keep your hands low at impact.

---

Feel confident as you stand over the ball.

---

With a downhill lie, align your shoulders with the slope.

As you follow through, touch the back of your left knee with your right knee.

---

Focus on solid contact with the driver.

---

Your arms and chest should move away together.

---

Maintain a consistent spine angle through the shot.

---

In downhill rough, use your most lofted wedge.

---

Rotate your forearms as you release the club.

Swing the club fluidly.

---

At the top of the backswing, point the shaft at the target.

---

For higher ball flight, put the ball more forward in your stance.

---

When hitting into the wind, use one more club and make a three-quarter finish.

---

Don't turn your shoulders too soon on the downswing.

---

With a downhill lie, flex your knees.

Don't pull the club back too far inside.

---

Your weight should be on the balls of your feet.

---

In fairway bunker, concentrate on hitting the ball first.

---

Open the clubface in tall grass.

---

For a draw, let your hands release after impact.

---

Take more club and swing within yourself.

Your left arm should fold after impact.

---

Turn your right hip and shoulder all the way through.

---

Set up with your head slightly behind the ball.

---

The divot should start just past where the ball was sitting.

---

Keep your weight on the inside of your right foot as you swing back.

Your shoulders should be behind the ball at the top of your swing.

---

Your right hip should turn through as you swing.

---

With the driver, don't hit down on the ball; sweep it.

---

Hit down on the ball with irons.

---

To cure a slice, close your shoulders more.

---

Don't break your wrists before impact.

---

Think "slow from the top."

---

Don't come up too soon after impact.

---

Feel a little tension in your left shoulder at the top.

---

Come through with your right arm, right shoulder and right hip.

---

Finish toward the target.

---

Try to get your power from your hips not from your arms.

---

Set up with your heels as far apart as your shoulders.

Lean to the right a little at set-up.

Relax at set-up....relax.

Keep your eyes level with the ground.

Hit through the ball.

Don't be too mechanical.

Stick your butt out a little.

Take a slightly wider stance when hitting in the wind.

Start the swing slowly and then accelerate.

As you swing down, point the butt of the club at the ball.

Your hip turn should be about half that of your shoulders.

Allow the hands to release after impact.

At address, turn your left foot out a little.

Hit the ball first and then the ground with irons.

---

Make a full turn with your back facing the target.

---

Get your right side through as you swing forward.

---

Finish with your chest facing the target.

---

Let your arms just drop with gravity.

---

Sweep the ball off the ground with a fairway wood.

---

In deep rough, swing down more steeply at the ball.

---

Stay balanced before, during and after your swing.

---

Keep your right elbow close to your right side on the downswing.

---

## Ramblings: Number 8 Mistake— Coiling and Uncoiling

The best way to make a golf swing is to simply uncoil. This assumes that that you are coiled in the first place. Very few amateurs actually coil when they take the club back. It is not difficult, but it is also not very natural.

The secret to coiling is to keep the right knee bent with most of your weight on your right leg. Then turn your hips as far as you can. This is coiling. Of course, you take the club back with your chest and arms, but the coil is in your legs. That is where your power is.

There is a tendency to want to straighten the right leg, but avoid this at all costs. If the right leg straightens, you can turn your hips farther around, but this is not what you want to do. The idea is not to turn your hips as far as possible; rather, the idea is to keep your right knee bent and turn your hips so that you are fully coiled. This is where your power comes from.

Once you're nicely coiled, your first move for the downswing is to bump your left hip slightly back and left. As you begin to uncoil, it is important to keep your right shoulder back. In other words, uncoil from the ground up, not from the shoulders down. The hips begin to uncoil, and then the shoulders uncoil.

If you do it right, it is truly wonderful and easy. The only caveat is that the uncoiling action is not particularly natural. I can't think of any other sports in which we uncoil our hips in such a way, perhaps baseball. So stick with it. Practice at home without a club. Once you get this move down you will be a very happy golfer.

Pretend that you are confident before every shot.

---

With the ball below your feet, bend more with your knees, not your back.

---

Try to keep a fluid tempo.

---

Don't slide to the right as you swing back.

---

Extend your right arm after impact.

---

With an uphill lie, set up with your shoulders parallel to the slope.

Choke down for shots in deep rough.

---

Your shoulders and arms should work together.

---

Do not slide the hips.

---

Turn your left shoulder over your right hip.

---

Have a nice, consistent rhythm to your swing.

---

Make a meaningful practice swing.

---

At the top, do not dip past parallel.

---

Grip the club lightly.

---

Widen your stance to hit a low shot into the wind.

---

Follow through completely on every shot.

---

Keep your spine angle constant in order to stay on plane.

---

Swing at only 80% of your strength.

---

Fire through with the right side.

---

Loosen your grip.

---

Don't sway when taking the club back.

---

Keep your wrists cocked as you come into the ball.

---

Keep your shoulders level on the takeaway, not dipped.

---

Come into the ball from the inside.

---

Turn your chest through impact.

---

The driver shaft should lean back at address.

Choke down on the club for
in-between yardage shots.

---

Visualize the face of the iron going
through the ball and toward the target.

---

Never flick at the ball with your wrists.

---

Set your hands forward on all irons.

---

Grip down for a punch shot.

---

Coil by moving your right buttock
back away from the ball.

Make a descending blow with your irons.

---

With a downhill lie, chase the ball down the hill with the club head.

---

Rotate around your spine on all shots.

---

With fairway woods, extend your arms down the target line.

---

Use a slower and smoother swing with long irons.

---

Commit to the shot.

---

Keep your back straight and bend from the hips.

---

Begin the downswing slowly.

---

Keep your chin up; it will keep your spine straight.

---

On a flop shot, keep your wrists cocked as long as possible.

---

Trust your swing on every shot.

---

Try taking a shorter backswing with the driver for accuracy.

---

On the backswing, keep your hands as far from your head as possible.

---

At impact, your hips should be more open than your shoulders.

---

Keep your weight on the inside of your right foot on the backswing.

---

Lay up to your preferred distance, say 100 yards.

---

Tee the ball up a little higher on your drives.

---

For more control with the driver, choke down an inch or two.

---

With a downhill lie, place the ball back in your stance.

---

On a downhill lie, try to swing very smoothly.

---

Hit down on the ball with a fairway wood.

---

Swing easier for more control with your driver.

---

Choke down on your short irons for greater control.

---

Start your swing by dropping, not turning, your right shoulder slightly.

Make sure to keep your head still when hitting wedges.

Over-swinging reduces your accuracy.

Accelerate through the ball on all shots.

Do not be tentative; commit to your swing.

Stick your butt out as you take the club back to the top.

Start your swing by bumping your hips slightly to the left.

Then rotate your right hip towards the target.

At contact, the back of your left hand should be just ahead of the ball.

Take the club back with your shoulders and arms as one unit.

At set-up, let your hands hang down naturally, then grip the club.

Pause briefly at the top.

Start down slowly and then accelerate.

On the takeaway, keep your left arm in close to your chest.

---

As your turn back, keep your right knee bent.

---

Open your mouth a little to reduce tension.

---

With irons, drive your right shoulder down and through the ball.

---

Grip the club in your fingers, not in your palm.

---

The angle of your bent right knee should stay the same throughout the swing.

Close the clubface a little in order to hit a draw.

As you swing, drive your right shoulder down and through.

Finish with your right shoulder over your left foot.

Swing smoothly when the ball is below your feet.

Hit through the ball when using the driver.

Move your arms and shoulders as one unit as you swing down.

---

Delay the release of the club head.

---

Do not stand up as you take the club back.

---

To get spin, trap the ball against the ground.

---

Take the club back with your body, not your hands.

---

Keep the lag in the club as long as you can.

---

When your body stops turning back, don't continue moving your arms.

---

On the takeaway, keep your hands as far from your right ear as possible.

---

Do not let the club unhinge on the way down.

---

Visualize yourself making a perfect swing.

---

Take one more club and swing easily with every iron.

---

Your weight should move off your front leg on the backswing.

---

Keep your right palm facing down through impact.

---

Accelerate through and then release the club.

---

To start the downswing, the hips should move before the shoulders.

---

Swing your hybrid club just like a 7 iron.

---

In the wind, take two clubs more and grip down.

---

In a fairway bunker, think about sweeping the ball.

---

Don't stop your shoulder turn too early.

---

Finish your swing in balance.

---

Never be afraid when hitting a golf shot; golf is *fun*.

---

If between clubs, simply choke down on the longer iron.

---

Always plant your feet solidly.

---

Turn your hips level; don't tilt them.

---

Relax at set-up; let your tension go.

Smack the ball with your right wrist at impact.

## Ramblings: Number 9 Mistake— Helping the Ball into the Air

Trying to help the ball into the air is especially problematic when there is something in front of you that you do not like, perhaps a water hazard. I was playing with a woman once who actually had a nice swing. When we played the hole with a water hazard up ahead, she proceeded to hit four balls into the water with her fairway wood. The idea is to hit *down* on the ball and then the ball will go *up*. This, of course, is counterintuitive. You have to trust the club.

The same is true for chipping. I played with another friend who hit chips that were low line drives—barely above the ground. He immediately blurts out: "I didn't get under it." No! You should never try to get the club *under* the ball with a chip. You hit *down* on the ball with the club and then the ball goes *up*. That's why the face of the club is slanted—it makes the ball go up! This takes some practice and you must learn to trust the club.

When setting up with the driver, your right shoulder should be lower than the left.

---

For a drive, your hands should be set up in front of your left thigh.

---

Bend from your hips, not your back. Don't try to steer the club.

---

The club should swoosh just passed the ball.

---

Play the ball back in your stance when hitting the driver off the deck.

---

Rotate your forearms as you hit through the ball.

---

Make a flatter approach with your 3 wood.

---

Keep your spine angle the same throughout the shot.

---

Finish hitting the ball before you look up.

---

Make a relaxed swing with short irons.

---

Make a slightly descending blow when hitting your irons.

---

For a lower ball flight, extend your arms down the line.

---

Always accelerate through impact.

---

Make a balanced and athletic stance when setting up.

---

Take only a three-quarter swing when hitting a ball from the rough.

---

The first downswing move should be lateral, without turning.

---

Keep your left arm relaxed and fairly straight on the backswing.

---

Your left wrist should face the target at impact.

---

To hit a higher shot, position the ball more forward in your stance.

---

Make a steeper swing than normal when hitting from the rough.

---

Keep your right elbow in on the downswing.

---

Take one more club when hitting from the rough.

---

Make a nice smooth swing when playing in the wind.

Stick your butt out on all shots.

---

Don't let your weight go outside your right foot during the backswing.

---

Keep your chin up to maintain the proper spine angle.

---

With an uphill lie, choke down and take one more club.

---

With a downhill lie, aim more to the left.

---

For a fade, play the ball slightly forward.

For a draw, play the ball slightly back in your stance.

---

Swing slower and smoothly when in the wind.

---

Tee the ball lower for more control with your driver.

---

Let your body turn through as you swing.

---

Swing smoothly and easily from fairway sand.

---

For more control, take the club back only three-fourths of a full swing.

Turn back with your shoulders; don't lift with your arms.

Don't bend over too much at address.

Put more weight on your left leg when hitting from the rough.

Take the club back slowly; there is no rush.

With irons, take a divot after hitting the ball.

Don't break your wrists too early on the downswing.

---

You should release the club with your turn, not with your hands.

---

Make a full turn back with your shoulders.

---

Don't flip the club head at the ball.

---

Think about compressing the ball when you make contact.

---

Your belt buckle should face the target at impact.

---

Set up for a hybrid shot with the ball inside your left heel.

Keep your knees bent and relaxed on important shots.

---

Swing down slowly from the top.

---

Choke down for more control on all clubs.

---

Keep your feet and legs quiet.

---

Don't take the driver back past parallel.

---

Drop your right elbow into your side on the downswing.

---

Maintain your posture as you begin your backswing.

---

Move the ball farther back in your stance for the higher lofted clubs.

---

Don't strangle the club; keep a nice light grip.

---

Take the club back by simply turning your shoulders.

---

Take one more club and swing smoothly and easily.

---

Slow from the top is a good way to start your tempo.

Make sure your feet are far enough apart, especially with the longer clubs.

---

The downswing should begin with the hips, not the arms.

---

The ball will go farther with good timing than with muscles.

---

Watch the ball closely as you make contact.

---

Your hands should be relaxed at impact.

For better accuracy, try taking your driver back only halfway.

---

Keep your left arm in against your chest as you turn back.

---

Many swing problems can be cured with a correct stance at set-up.

---

Stick your butt out to maintain your spine angle.

---

Never swing at 100% power; stay within yourself.

---

To hit a higher shot, open the clubface and open your stance.

---

Relax and enjoy the game. Nobody really cares where your golf ball goes.

## Practicing

Never hit more than three shots in a row with the same club at the range.

---

Practice hitting shots from bad lies and from divots.

---

Hit 20 putts from 3 or 4 feet from all four sides of the hole.

---

Hit ten lag putts from 20 to 25 feet.

---

Practice swinging with your feet together to develop the right release.

Learn the distance for each wedge swinging back only to the 9 o'clock position.

Aim for a specific target with every practice shot.

Practice your chip shots every chance you get.

Speed is more important than line on putts; practice speed for distance control.

Make up putting games to keep practice interesting.

If your concentration is diminishing, stop practicing.

---

Practice long lag putts; they are the most important.

---

Try the cross-handed grip for a change when putting.

---

Swing from 9 o'clock back to 3 o'clock forward to learn the basic swing.

---

Practice hitting your driver with a half swing to keep arms and body in synch.

---

Practice hitting 15-foot to 20-foot putts so that they all go past the hole by 2 feet.

Swing from 9 o'clock with your hands apart to learn how to release the club.

After a round, practice hitting the shots that were the most troublesome.

Chip with a sand wedge from all around the green.

Practice putts from the 12 points of a clock around a hole.

Practice using a one-handed swing with your right arm.

Practice your putts and chips every time you go to the range.

Before starting a round, practice playing the first three holes at the driving range.

Swing at 50% speed when learning a new swing idea.

Pull your right foot back to practice swinging with a good release.

Practice hitting your 5 iron the same distance as your 7 iron.

Always make a full finish with every practice swing.

Make one-handed swings to find your rhythm.

---

Practice chipping with a hybrid club and use a putting stroke.

---

Try hitting from divots to develop confidence in this shot.

---

Practice hitting from sand with your 9 iron to get more distance.

---

Practice pitches with 8 o'clock, 9 o'clock, and 10 o'clock backswings.

---

Practice 3-foot and 4-foot putts extensively.

---

Check your set-up posture in front of a mirror.

---

Practice your swing in super slow motion.

---

Swing with your right arm only to practice the correct weight shift.

---

Take one or two practice swings before every shot you hit on the range.

---

Take notes on what you learned at the range.

---

Practice hitting your driver a variety of distances with a full swing.

## Ramblings: Number 10 Mistake—Not Having Enough Fun

It was a beautiful sunny Sunday in Seattle and I was driving across the floating bridge to go golfing with friends. I had played golf the day before and shot an excellent score, well, at least excellent for me. I had a great day and I was very pleased. What if I did not play as well today? What if I double bogeyed the first two holes? Then my score would be lousy. I would be ruined for the day.

This really started to bother me and I was becoming quite trepidatious. What could I do? I drove on, puzzled and a bit worried. I realized that some shots will be good, many will be mediocre, a handful will be really lousy and a few will be spectacular. That is golf, right? And the score will be what the score will be.

The sun was out; the convertible top was down and I was contemplating this infernal game. I realized that I should just try my hardest on each shot and that was all I could do. Focus on trying to hit each shot the best I could. I certainly cared about the result but I could not *control* the result. All I could control was how I hit the ball.

So, that was my plan. I focused simply on hitting the golf ball. Guess what? I actually hit the ball pretty well. Not as good as the previous day, but better than normal. But more importantly, I had fun. I enjoyed being with my friends. I enjoyed being outside on a nice day.

No one cared what my golf score was…not my wife, not my kids, not my mother and not my friends. OK, I suppose I did care a bit, but I learned a good lesson. All I can do is hit the ball so I should just concentrate on hitting the ball. And the cool thing about golf…the ball always goes exactly where I hit it!

We golfers need to have more fun. No one cares what your score is. Golf is an extremely difficult game. And you are not that good! So, no more whining, no more bitching and no bad attitude.

Figure out a way to have fun on the course.

Funny story, and true: One of my friends plays golf only when she goes to Lake Tahoe. She is a terrible golfer. If she played 18 holes she would probably shoot 140. She only plays nine, however. We were playing one day and as we walked off the first green her husband was writing down the score. "I got a 16," she said. "I'll put you down for a 9," he replied. "No, I had a 16. I want to keep track and see how good I do. I want to see if I can beat my score from last week." Wow, I thought, unbelievable! But she was having fun and her goals were relative only to herself.

We did have a very enjoyable round of golf. Afterwards, we walked to the clubhouse with smiles and good attitudes. When is the last time you did that after shooting a 16 on one hole?

## More Information

Please visit our web site for more information about quantity discounts and golf merchandise:

www.swingthoughts-sissies.com

You may order books in quantities directly from us. See the web site for details.

Made in the USA
Charleston, SC
11 April 2014